**Replacement costs will be
billed after 42 days overdue.**

FRANKLIN PARK PUBLIC LIBRARY
FRANKLIN PARK, ILL.

Each borrower is held responsible for all library
material drawn on his card and for fines
accruing on the same. No material will be
issued until such fine has been paid.

All injuries to library material beyond
reasonable wear and all losses shall be made
good to the satisfaction of the librarian.

Pebble™

Woodland Animals

Wolves

by William John Ripple

Consulting Editor: Gail Saunders-Smith, PhD
Consultant: The International Wolf Center
Ely, Minnesota

Capstone
press

Mankato, Minnesota

Pebble Books are published by Capstone Press,
151 Good Counsel Drive, P.O. Box 669, Mankato, Minnesota 56002.
www.capstonepress.com

1 2 3 4 5 6 11 10 09 08 07 06

Library of Congress Cataloging-in-Publication Data
Ripple, William John.
    Wolves / by William John Ripple.
    p. cm.—(Pebble Books. Woodland animals)
    Summary: "Simple text and photographs introduce the habitat, appearance and
behavior of wolves"—Provided by publisher.
    Includes bibliographical references and index.
    ISBN-13: 978-0-7368-4247-1 (hardcover)
    ISBN-10: 0-7368-4247-0 (hardcover)
    1. Wolves—Juvenile literature. I. Title. II. Series.
QL737.C22R54 2006
599.773—dc22   2004028429

Note to Parents and Teachers

The Woodland Animals set supports national science standards related to life science. This book describes and illustrates wolves. The photographs support early readers in understanding the text. The repetition of words and phrases helps early readers learn new words. This book also introduces early readers to subject-specific vocabulary words, which are defined in the Glossary. Early readers may need assistance to read some words and to use the Table of Contents, Glossary, Read More, Internet Sites, and Index sections of the book.

Table of Contents

What Are Wolves?

Wolves are
large mammals.
Wolves look like big dogs.

Thick fur keeps
wolves warm.
Wolves are black,
brown, gray, or white.

areas where wolves live

Where Wolves Live

Wolves live in North America, Europe, and Asia. Wolves live in forests, grasslands, deserts, and the Arctic.

Body Parts

Wolves have
long, furry tails.
Their tails keep them warm.

Wolves have strong jaws
to help them eat
meat and bones.

Wolf Packs

Most wolves live in
family groups called packs.

Wolves howl to call their pack together.

The pack hunts together.
They eat deer, elk, moose,
and other animals.

The pack curls up
and sleeps near each other.

Glossary

Arctic—a cold area near the North Pole; some wolves live in the Arctic.

desert—a dry area of land with few plants

forest—land covered mostly by trees; forests are also called woodlands.

grasslands—a large area of mostly flat land covered by grass and other small plants

howl—a long, loud call; wolves howl for many reasons; wolves sometimes howl to defend their territory or to let other animals know where they are.

hunt—to find and kill animals for food

mammal—a warm-blooded animal with a backbone and hair or fur; female mammals feed milk to their young.

pack—a family of wolves that lives and hunts together; wolf packs usually have 5 to 12 wolves.

22

Read More

Economos, Christine. *Wolves*. Science Links. Philadelphia: Chelsea Clubhouse, 2003.

Spilsbury, Richard, and Louise Spilsbury. *A Pack of Wolves*. Animal Groups. Chicago: Heinemann Library, 2003.

Internet Sites

FactHound offers a safe, fun way to find Internet sites related to this book. All of the sites on FactHound have been researched by our staff.

Here's how:

1. Visit *www.facthound.com*
2. Type in this special code **0736842470** for age-appropriate sites. Or enter a search word related to this book for a more general search.
3. Click on the **Fetch It** button.

FactHound will fetch the best sites for you!

Index

Word Count: 95
Grade Level: 1
Early-Intervention Level: 10

Editorial Credits

Mari C. Schuh, editor; Patrick D. Dentinger, set designer; Ted Williams,
    book designer; Wanda Winch, photo researcher; Scott Thoms, photo editor

Photo Credits

Bruce Coleman Inc./Erwin and Peggy Bauer, 16
Creatas, 14
Minden Pictures/Konrad Wothe, cover
Tom and Pat Leeson, 4, 6, 8, 10, 12, 18, 20
U.S. Fish and Wildlife Service/Gary Kramer, 1

The author dedicates this book to his nephew Kail Vaith and niece Lindzie Vaith
of Lesterville, South Dakota.